35+ PROJECTS

Crafting WITH
MASON JARS
AND OTHER GLASS CONTAINERS

Over **35** *simple and beautiful upcycling projects*

HESTER VAN OVERBEEK

CICO BOOKS
LONDON NEW YORK

For my parents Anton and Hendrikje,
my biggest craft fans

Published in 2016 by CICO Books
An imprint of Ryland Peters & Small Ltd
20–21 Jockey's Fields   341 E 116th St
London WC1R 4BW   New York, NY 10029

www.rylandpeters.com

10 9 8 7 6 5 4 3 2 1

A CIP catalog record for this book is available from
the Library of Congress and the British Library.

ISBN: 978 1 78249 329 7

Printed in China

Editor: Gillian Haslam
Designer: Geoff Borin
Photographer: James Gardiner
Illustrator: Jasmine Parker
Template illustrations: Hester van Overbeek
Stylist: Hester van Overbeek

In-house editor: Anna Galkina
Art director: Sally Powell
Production controller: Sarah Kulasek-Boyd
Publishing manager: Penny Craig
Publisher: Cindy Richards

CONTENTS

INTRODUCTION

When I told friends the subject of my new book, they responded "35+ things to do with a jar? Surely it's 'fill with jam' or 'put flowers in' and that's it!" However, I didn't struggle at all when compiling the project ideas as jars are so versatile. My problem was limiting myself to the 39 ideas shown in this book.

Mason jars and jam jars have been "having a moment" for some time now, but you always see them used in a very romantic, girly kind of way. I decided I would like to show you that jars can be used in a more contemporary fashion as well. I have devised jar projects for every occasion, to use as decorative objects in your home (such as the mini terrariums seen on the right), to use for food and drinks, to give your garden a bit more style, and even turned them into lights. All projects are explained step by step and have great artworks to show you exactly what to do. You might think glass is tricky to work with, but with the right tools and safety precautions, it really isn't that difficult. Still not sure? There are also many projects that don't involve using power tools, like the candle votive projects and the vases.

For those of you who are familiar with my website www.hestershandmadehome.com and previous book, *Furniture Hacks*, you will know I like upcycling, reusing, or simply using what I have lying around. It's not just a budget consideration—it also makes so much more sense to use what you already have instead of buying new materials. Jars are the perfect example of this—you have them in your larder or stacked up on your shelves, so instead of putting them out for recycling, why not give them a new lease of life as a coffee cup or bird feeder? Follow my lead and start using your jars in a stylish way!

Happy crafting!

Hester xx

Collecting jars

You know how some people select their wine depending on the label? Well, I choose my groceries depending on how useful the jar will be when it's empty! Standard clear jam or jelly jars are easy to find, but there are also some amazingly shaped and colored jars out there, especially if you venture into the foreign food aisles in the supermarket or shop at an organic grocery store.

I've always collected jars so I have a ready stash when I have a crafting urge or want to make jam, but in preparation for this book I had to source a lot of jars. So there I was at the local supermarket, scanning the shelves for the prettiest jars around, not looking at the jar contents (we had some crazy meals in those weeks!).

Preserving jars

Since the invention of the Mason jar in 1858, the glass jar has been a staple in every household as it made preserving fruit and vegetables a lot easier. The Mason jar is a wide-mouthed molded glass jar, that has screw threads on the outside of its neck to fit a metal ring. This metal ring presses down a separate steel disc to hermetically seal the jar when it's screwed closed. By the early 20th century, industrial advances made jar manufacturing easier and faster and the Ball brothers (who started their business with glass jars in 1886) were mass-producing their jars in the USA.

In Europe, there were other well-known brands, such as the German Weck jar—with a Weck jar, the glass lids are kept securely in place with steel tension clips and a separate rubber seal. In the UK, John Kilner produced his first Kilner jar toward the end of the 19th century, and this brand is still produced today, in a large variety of shapes and sizes, all with screw and clip tops. You can find all these brands and more used in the projects in this book.

Where to buy

Ball Mason jars are widely available in the USA; if you live in the UK try Lakeland or eBay for these jars. The Weck brand is widely available in Europe, as are Kilner jars. Old-fashioned kitchen stores are always good places to pick up preserving jars, but as these become more and more popular in craft projects, the jars are becoming easier to buy in grocery stores and supermarkets.

Flea markets, car boot sales, and yard sales are also great places for sourcing jars. I once found a box of vintage Mason jars in my local charity shop and bought some of them with the small change I had in my pockets. When I returned from the ATM a few minutes later, they were all gone. You have to be quick when you spot some good jars!

If you do buy old jars, there are websites where you can check whether the jar you have is vintage or collectable. Google the make of your jar and look at how the brand name is written to check how old your jar is. You don't want to start drilling into a very valuable jar!

Basic techniques

Drilling into glass

I use a rotary cutter for drilling into glass, as it has a variable speed and is easy to control. You might think it's tricky drilling into glass, but if you take these tips into account it really isn't that hard at all! You may want to practise drilling on a spare jar first.

1 Work slowly—don't rush when drilling into a jar or you will break it. Keep your rotary cutter or drill on a low speed and don't press it down on the glass too hard.

2 Keep it cool—have running water close by to cool the glass and drill tip. When the glass is heated by the friction of drilling, there is a greater chance of it cracking and breaking. You could also use a cooling gel (some drill bits are sold with a little bottle of this gel). I place my jar in the kitchen sink on top of an old towel (which keeps it steady), so every now and then I can stop drilling and run the jar under the tap. I use a cordless drill—if using one with a power cord, take great care not to have the drill anywhere close to water (for this reason, I always recommend using a cordless one).

3 Use the correct drill bit—a diamond tip cutter gives the best result and the fastest cut.

4 Always wear safety goggles, safety gloves, and a dust mask when drilling into glass. If you have long hair, tie it out of the way. Don't wear garments with long, loose sleeves.

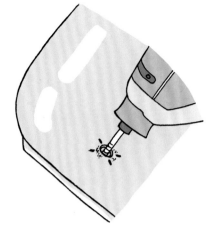

How to drill

Using a felt-tip pen, mark the place on the glass where you want to drill. Place the rotary cutter on the mark and slowly drill the hole. If you need the hole to be larger than the width of your drill bit, slowly start moving the drill around inside the hole, making the cut bigger with every turn or wiggle until you have the necessary width.

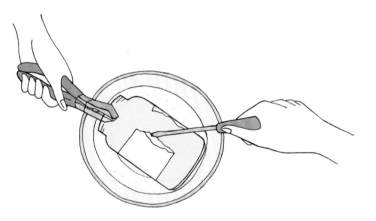

Removing labels from jars

If you are reusing jam or jelly jars or drinks bottles, you will probably need to remove the sticky labels. The quickest way to do this is to submerge the jar in a bowl of very hot water and dishwashing liquid. Let the jar sit in the bowl for a few minutes, then push and ease the label off using a knife or an implement with a flat edge, such as a screwdriver or palette knife. Hold the jar steady with tongs or pliers, as you don't want to scald your hands in the hot water. Rinse the jar clean and scrub off any remaining sticky residue with a dishwashing sponge.

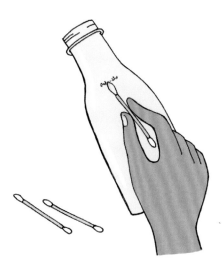

Removing "best before" dates

"Best before" or "use by" dates are easily removed using a cotton swab drenched in nail polish remover. Rub it over the printed date and it will quickly disappear.

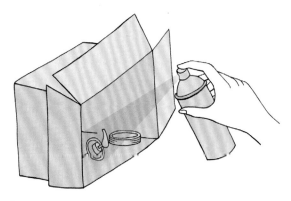

Spray paint

Spray painting should always be done in a well-ventilated room or outside. I like to create a little spray-paint booth from an empty cardboard box placed on its side, as this stops the fine mist of paint going everywhere. Place your item in the box and give it a light coat of paint. The walls of the box will make sure the paint won't go on any other surfaces. Apply a second coat if necessary.

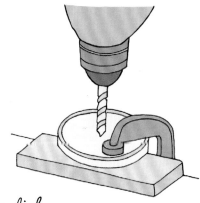

Drilling a lid

When drilling the lid of a jar, secure the lid to your work surface with a G clamp. This is especially important with Mason jar lids as they are really thin and can start spinning when you put the drill on them, risking the possibility of you being cut by the spinning lid. Tie up long hair and push sleeves up before you use your drill. Put a spare piece of wood between your lid and your work surface so that you do not drill into the tabletop. Secure the lid to the wood and the table with the G clamp. Mark the spot where you want the hole to be and place your drill on top.

Crafting WITH MASON JARS

AND OTHER GLASS CONTAINERS

Chapter 2

DECORATE YOUR HOME

Yarn-wrapped VASE

I love making this chunky yarn, and it's a great way to use up leftover fabric scraps. The yarn can be used in all kinds of ways—make big balls and display them as decorative objects, crochet with it, or upcycle a glass jar, as shown here. You can transform all kinds of jars into stylish vases, such as milk bottles or little tea light holders. I used cotton fabric for this project, but the yarn looks great made from silks too. Just make sure the fabrics you choose are all of the same thickness, so select either silks or cottons rather than a combination of both.

YOU WILL NEED:

cotton fabric, cut into strips ¾ in (2cm) wide and in a variety of lengths

fabric scissors

glass jar

glue gun

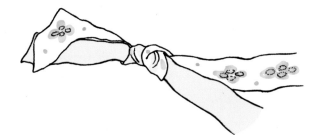

1 Knot two pieces of fabric together to start the yarn.

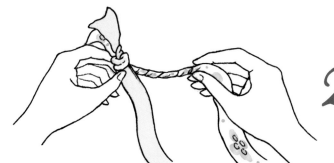

2 Hold one piece of fabric between your fingers and twist it away from you.

3 Pull the twisted piece toward you, taking it over the flat piece of fabric.

4 Pull the flat piece away from you and twist it between your fingers, as you did in step 2, then pull it toward you, placing it over the other piece. Continue until you reach the end of one of your pieces of cotton, following the sequence of twisting the fabric and pulling it over the other piece.

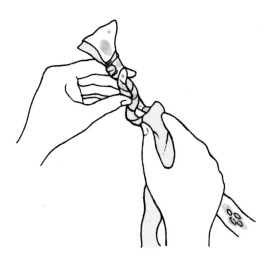

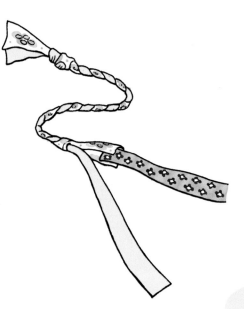

5 When you reach the end of a length of fabric, add another piece by folding it inside the existing piece. Keep twisting the fabric until your yarn is long enough to cover your chosen jar.

TIP
By cutting your fabric strips to different lengths, you will ensure the joins between pieces of fabric do not line up, making for a stronger yarn.

6 To attach the yarn to the jar, use the glue gun to apply little dots of hot glue to the jar. Remember that the glue dries quickly, so only apply glue to the lower part of the jar to begin with. Press the yarn into the glue and hold it in place for a moment to make sure it adheres correctly.

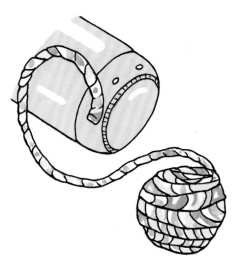

7 Continue to wind the yarn around the jar, applying more glue as necessary.

8 When you reach the top of the jar, cover the top rim with yarn to hide all the glass. Cut the yarn and ensure that any loose ends of fabric are firmly glued in place.

Natural room scents

Fragrances can provoke powerful memories, reminding you of an amazing place, a special person, or a particularly happy time in your life. Store-bought room scents are often synthetic fragrances—they do the job, but wouldn't it be nicer to have a natural alternative, blended with your own favorite scents?

Herbs, citrus fruit, and spices make great aromatic infusions. You can mix them in advance and store them in the fridge or freezer (great if you have a surplus of home-grown herbs). When you're ready to use them, simply place the jar on a teapot warmer and wait for the room to be filled with the smells of summer.

YOU WILL NEED:

selection of citrus fruits, herbs, and whole spices

chopping board and knife

large preserving jars

water

teapot warmer with a tea light

Select the raw ingredients for your room scent. My favorite combinations are lemon/rosemary, orange/cinnamon/star anise, and lime/thyme/mint.

Cut the fruit into slices and arrange in the preserving jar. Add sprigs of fresh herbs and any spices.

Fill the jar with water and place on the teapot warmer, over a lit tea light.

TIP

If you do store the scents in the fridge, it's a good idea to warm the contents gently on the stove first, otherwise it will take ages for the little tea light to heat the water. Tip the contents of the jar into a small saucepan and heat until warm. Pour back into the jar and place on the teapot warmer.

Glue-patterned VASE

Tall, skinny jars are great to use as vases and they are very easy to transform into something special using just a glue gun and some spray paint. You simply "write" on the glass using the hot glue—this might take some practise, but you'll quickly master the art of creating raised letters with the glue. If you don't fancy letters, why not draw an abstract pattern on the jar, or make small polka dots with the hot glue—be as creative as you wish!

YOU WILL NEED:

piece of paper

pen

tall, narrow skinny jar (I used a pasta sauce jar)

masking tape

glue gun

toothpick

newspaper

spray paint

1 Decide how you want to decorate your jar. I wrote the word "Flowers," but you can choose any words you like. "Love" and "Home" always work well, or for a gift, write the name of the person receiving your bouquet of flowers. Write the word on a piece of paper, place it inside the jar in the correct position, and secure with masking tape.

2 Balance the jar in the roll of masking tape, as this holds it at a convenient and stable angle. Using the glue gun, start tracing over the letters. The key to success is to work slowly. Hot glue can be tricky to work with, so try to be as precise as possible.

3   The glue gun always leaves fine wisps of glue, so remove as many of these as possible using the toothpick. Allow the glue to cool down (this only takes a few seconds). Remove the paper from inside.

4   Place the jar outside or in a well-ventilated room. Cover work surfaces with newspaper, or place inside a box (see page 11). Spray the jar all over with spray paint. Let the paint dry, then spray a second coat. Let dry thoroughly before using.

Etched JAR

There are two methods for etching glass—you can use a tool like an engraving pen or rotary multi-tool to scrape away small areas of glass, or you can use a chemical etching cream which removes a thin layer of glass. I like using my rotary tool as I feel more in control and I prefer not to use chemicals. Simple engravers are not expensive to buy, and think of all the personalized presents you can make!

I love Scandinavian style and one of its most famous folk-style images is the Dala horse. As I live by the coast and have seagull images everywhere, I thought it would be fun to etch a Dala seagull.

YOU WILL NEED:

glass jar

seagull template
(see page 124)

tape

old towel

engraving pen or
rotary cutter with
an engraving bit

safety goggles and
gloves

1 Copy the seagull template, enlarging or reducing it to suit the size of your jar. Tape the template to the inside of the jar.

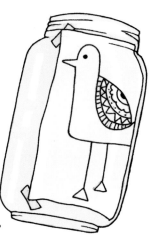

2 Place the jar on an old folded towel, to keep it steady while you etch. I use a brightly colored towel as this makes it easier to see which areas of glass have been etched.

3 Following the instructions provided with your engraving pen, first etch the outline of the seagull. When this is complete, etch the patterned wing. Remove the paper template and fill in the body, using short strokes of the engraving pen.

4 When the seagull is complete, wash the jar thoroughly to remove any glass dust.

TIP

Always wear safety goggles and gloves when you are etching glass.

Coffee cup JAR

When I think of camping, I immediately picture campfires, cups of coffee, and toasting marshmallows, sitting around the fire, dressed in a plaid shirt, listening to somebody strum the guitar while looking at the mountains in the distance! To get a little piece of this outdoor lifestyle in my own backyard, I created this jar sleeve with a handle. I love the leather sleeve—it keeps your drink warm and it's pretty easy to make, but you do need a few tools, like a hole puncher and rivets; or you can simply glue a wooden handle to a Mason jar instead (see page 49).

YOU WILL NEED:

jar

tape measure

piece of leather

pencil

craft knife

metal straight edge

cutting mat

hole punch

4 rivets

rivet anvil and setting tool

hammer

1 Measure your jar from the base to bottom of the rim — for my jar, that's a height of 2¾in (7cm). Also measure the circumference by wrapping your tape measure around the jar — for my jar, that's 9½in (24cm).

2 Using these measurements, draw out your sleeve on the back of the leather. You need a 2¾in (7cm) overlap on the circumference, so for my jar I drew a rectangle 12¼ x 2¾in (31 x 7cm). Using the craft knife and metal straight edge on the cutting mat, cut out this rectangle.

3 Make a mark 1¼in (3cm) in from one end on both top and bottom long edges. On the short edge, measure and mark ¾in (2cm) from each corner. Connect the dots to create an envelope shape.

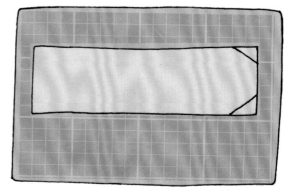

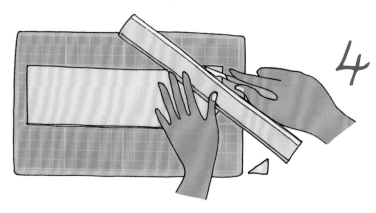

4 Using the craft knife on the cutting mat, cut off the corner triangles.

5 Cut a strip of leather measuring 1 x 5¼ in (2.5 x 13cm) for the handle.

6 Measure to find the middle of the sleeve (don't count the overlap), and on the back mark two dots ½ in (1cm) from the top and bottom edges. Using the correct size hole in the hole punch for the rivets, punch a hole on the marked spots.

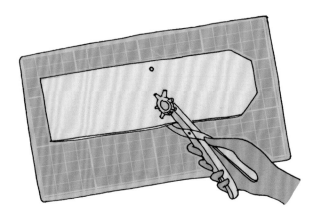

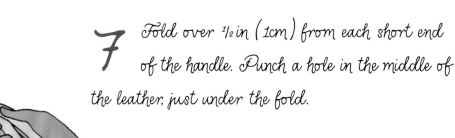

7 Fold over ½ in (1cm) from each short end of the handle. Punch a hole in the middle of the leather, just under the fold.

8 Position the handle on the sleeve. Push a rivet post through the sleeve and the handle, top with its cap, and hammer it closed using the setting tool and with the anvil block beneath the leather. Repeat for the other hole to attach the handle.

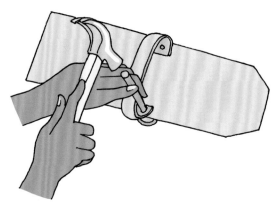

9 Punch two holes in the envelope end of the sleeve.

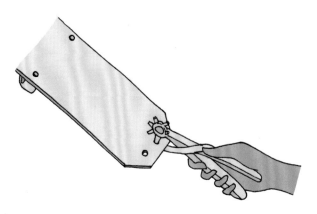

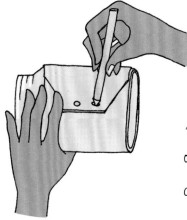

10 Wrap the sleeve around the jar as tightly as possible (this is to ensure the jar won't slip out of the leather sleeve). Using a pencil, mark where the corresponding holes will go on the leather.

11 Punch the two holes. Push the rivet post through the leather sleeve and the envelope flap, top with its cap, and hammer in place as before. Repeat with the other hole, then insert your jar, and brew some coffee!

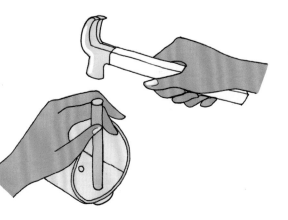

Wooden handle jar

This wooden handle option couldn't be simpler as it's a drawer handle glued to the jar. As well as the jar, you'll need a wooden drawer handle no wider then the height of the jar and a tube of superglue. Mark on the jar where you want your handle to go, apply superglue to the handle, and glue in place. Hold for 30 seconds until the glue has set. You could wrap a piece of masking tape around the handle and jar to hold it in place while the glue finishes drying. This cup is hand-wash only, as the glue would loosen in a dishwasher.

Hanging PLANTERS

Vertical gardens are a great way to add plants to even the smallest of living rooms and balconies. Taking up only a tiny amount of space, you can add as many levels to this planter as you wish. Filled with succulents, this would look great in your living room, or you could plant with herbs such as thyme and mint for a kitchen planter, or why not use brightly colored flowers for a vertical garden on your terrace? Just make sure your jars are wider at the rim then they are at the bottom, otherwise they will slip through the wooden holders. If you want to hang your vertical garden outside, make sure you choose a wood that has been weather-treated, such as the ridged decking boards I used here.

YOU WILL NEED:

plank of wood 18 in (45cm) long and 4¾ in (12cm) wide

measuring tape

pencil

3 x 17 fl oz (500ml) jars that are wider at the top than bottom (I used Weck preserving jars)

pair of compasses

drill with wood bit

jigsaw

sandpaper

paint

paintbrush

20 feet (6m) narrow rope

masking tape

small pebbles

potting compost

3 plants

1 On the plank of wood, draw three pencil lines 6 in (15cm), 12 in (30cm), and 18 in (45cm) from one end. (If using ridged wood as I have done, work on the plain side.) These will eventually become the three levels, but it is easier to keep the plank in one piece to saw out the circles and then cut into three pieces later.

2 Measure the circumference of the jar about 1 in (2.4cm) below the rim. To calculate the radius of the circle you need to cut in the wood, divide the circumference by 3.14 (this number is known as "pi"), and then divide by 2. Make a note of this measurement.

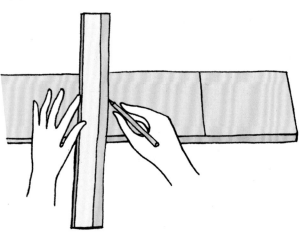

TIP

Don't be tempted to skip steps 2 and 3 and simply draw around the jar rim onto the wood. This would result in a hole that is too large, and your jars would simply slip through.

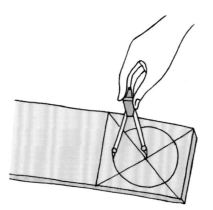

3 Find the middle of each of the three sections of wood by drawing two diagonal pencil lines from corner to corner. Fit a pencil into the compass and set the distance between pencil and compass point to the measurement you noted at the end of step 2. Place the point of the compass where the diagonal pencil lines cross and draw a circle. Repeat in the two remaining sections of wood.

TIP

If you don't have a pair of compasses, you can improvise by using a pencil with a piece of string tied around it. Use a thumbtack to anchor the string at the point where the diagonal lines cross. The length of string needs to correspond to the measurement noted at the end of step 2.

4 Drill a hole in the circle to fit your jigsaw blade through, then cut out the first circle. Repeat to cut out the two remaining circles.

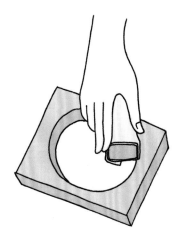

5 Cut the plank of wood along the vertical lines into the three sections. Smooth all rough edges with sandpaper.

6 Paint the three pieces of wood. I used a seagull gray as the color offsets the green plants nicely. Let dry, and apply a second coat if necessary.

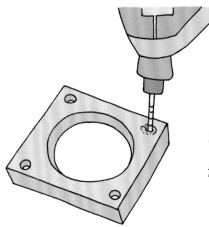

7 You need to drill a hole in each corner of the wood to push the hanging rope through. Mark the position in pencil, about ½ in (1cm) from each corner. Make sure the holes are large enough to accommodate the rope.

8 Cut four pieces of rope, each 5 feet (1.5m) in length. Wrap each of the cut ends in masking tape to prevent them fraying.

9 Push the rope through one of the pieces of wood and make a knot in the end. Repeat with the remaining three pieces of rope.

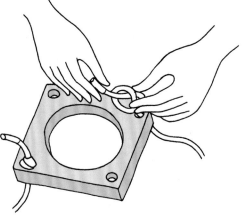

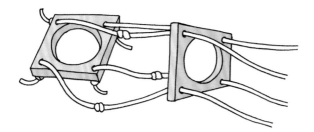

10 Measure 8 in (20cm) from the threaded piece of wood and make another knot in each piece of rope. Thread on the second piece of wood. Knot the rope and thread on the third piece of wood in the same way.

11 When all three pieces of wood are in place, knot the four lengths of rope together securely 12 in (30cm) from their top ends. Remove the masking tape from the rope ends.

12 Fill the bottom of the jars with a thin layer of pebbles—this helps with water drainage as the containers don't have holes in the bottom. Add a layer of potting compost on top of the pebbles and place your plants in the jars, filling around them with more potting compost and pressing it in firmly.

13 Place the planted jars in their wooden holders and hang your vertical garden from a curtain pole or a hanging basket hanger.

Milk bottle LIGHT

With a great lampshade and a light fitting, you can transform an empty milk bottle into a stylish table lamp in no time! Electric flex covered in colored cloth wire is now widely available and it adds a pop of color to this otherwise plain glass bottle. The size of your milk bottle determines the size of the lampshade—don't use a shade which is too large or your lamp will topple over. This project requires a wired light fitting—if you have no experience working with wiring, please ask an electrician as it's better to be safe then sorry.

1 Make sure your light fitting fits in the neck of your milk bottle. The base of the fitting needs to drop down inside the bottle while the remainder sits on the rim.

YOU WILL NEED:

milk bottle

plastic light fitting

rotary cutter with a diamond drill bit

cloth-covered electric flex with plug and light switch attached (widely available online)

white or transparent strain relief

superglue

masking tape

screwdriver

lampshade

light bulb

2 Referring to page 10, drill a hole in the bottle ¾ in (2cm) from the bottom and wide enough to fit the strain relief (this prevents the wire being pulled out of the fitting if you yank the cable too hard). I find it easiest to place the bottle in the kitchen sink, keeping it steady on a damp towel. Drill the hole on a low speed and don't put any pressure on the bottle. Keep the bottle cool with water to reduce the chances of the glass cracking.

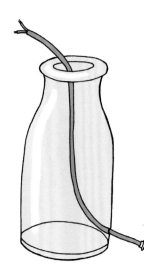

3 Push the electric flex through the strain relief, through the drilled hole, and up through the bottle neck. Ask a qualified electrician to wire the flex to the light fitting.

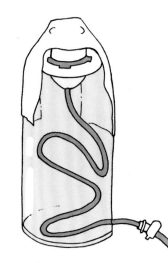

4 Glue the light fitting into the bottle opening using superglue, making sure it is level. Use a bit of masking tape to keep the fitting in place while the glue dries.

TIP
I transformed my plain lampshade by doodling a white graphic pattern all over it using a fabric-marker pen.

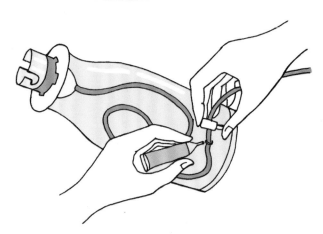

5 Make sure you have enough wire inside the milk bottle to create an attractive looped shape, then glue the strain relief to the bottle using superglue. Use a piece of masking tape to hold the strain relief in place while the glue dries. When the glue has set, tighten the screw of the strain relief.

6 Attach the lampshade and screw in the light bulb.

Knotted COVER

The appearance of a Mason jar is easily changed with a yarn cover—you could knit one, crochet one, or knot a cover, as shown here. To give the jar a modern edge, I used paracord —this is a great material to work with and it comes in a huge variety of colors. I use the jar as a decorative object, but you could use it as a vase or as a lantern by putting a tea light inside.

1 Measure the height of your jar. You will need to cut ten lengths of cord, with each length seven times the jar's height. My jar measures 7 in (18cm) high, so I cut the cord into 49-in (126-cm) lengths.

2 Also cut an 8-in (20-cm) piece of cord — this is the base ring. Carefully heat the cut ends with a lighter for a few seconds and press together while hot to make a circle (you can press with pliers or use your fingers).

YOU WILL NEED:

Mason jar, or similar large jar

tape measure

paracord (I used approximately 14 yards/13m)

scissors

lighter

pliers (optional)

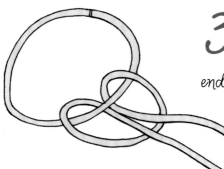

3 Fold one of your lengths of cord in half, place the folded end under the base ring, and push the ends through the loop to knot the cord on the base ring.

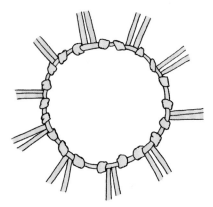

4 Attach the other nine lengths of cord in the same way, making sure they are evenly spaced around the base ring.

5 Place the jar on top of the base ring, with the knotted cords fanning out. Take the left cord of one piece and knot it to the right cord of its clockwise neighbor (see the detail diagrams on the far right for how to tie the knot).

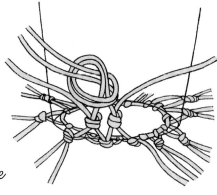

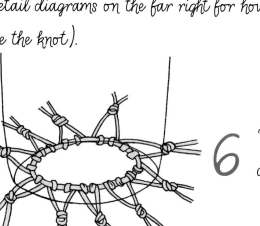

6 Working clockwise, knot each cord to its neighbor in this way.

7 With your first round of knots in place, continue with a second round in exactly the same way. Make sure the cover is knotted tightly around the jar.

8 Keep knotting the cords until you reach the top of the jar — I did five rounds of knots on my jar.

9 Cut the ends of the cords 1¼ in (3cm) from the final knot. Heat the ends with a lighter for a few seconds and press together to create a little loop (press with pliers or your fingers).

10 Cut another 8-in (20-cm) piece of cord and push it through the loops you have just created. Pull this drawstring up as tightly as you can around the neck of the jar and knot the ends together. Trim the ends of the cord ¼ in (5mm) from the knot.

Mini terrarium

One of the best ways to use a large jar is to transform it into a terrarium. I love succulents and they have made a real comeback recently. What better way to display them than with fun pink flamingos and decorative white sand—a mini beach scene for your table! In the smaller jar, a gold-painted dinosaur roars out from a succulent forest—I think the little ones in your life will appreciate this one. Make sure your jar is big enough for your plant to grow, so search the supermarket shelves for the biggest jar they have!

YOU WILL NEED:

large glass jars

pebbles

potting compost

small plants, such as succulents

decorative fine white sand

small pebbles or gravel

little ornaments

Start by placing a layer of pebbles in the base of your jar —this will help with drainage and will prevent the potting compost becoming waterlogged.

Put a layer of potting compost on top and position your plants. Top with more potting compost, firming it in around the base of the plant, then add a layer of decorative sand or pebbles.

Place your chosen ornaments around the plants for a whimsical effect.

Water the plants very carefully, trying not to disturb the sand or pebbles. Succulents and cacti make a good plant choice as they require little watering.

QUICK IDEAS

Paper vase COVER

Turn a standard glass jar into a retro-style vase with this paper cover. The monochrome look allows the flowers to stand out and inject your room with a bit of fun. You can use your own design or simply trace the template on page 125. I used handmade paper for my cover as its texture adds an extra dimension to the project, although the little lumps and bumps in the paper do make it a bit more difficult to draw super straight lines. If you are a neat freak, you might want to opt for a smooth machine-made paper.

YOU WILL NEED:

template (see page 125)

2 sheets of white handmade paper, A4 size or roughly 8¼ x 11¾ in (210 x 297mm)

low-tack sticking tape

black felt-tip pen

scissors

glass jar

needle

sewing thread, to match the color of the paper

1 Photocopy the template on page 125. The vase drawing needs to fit on the paper you are using, so you may need to enlarge or reduce it slightly. Alternatively, you can draw your own design.

2 Trace the template on to both sheets of paper. I find it easiest to do this by sticking the template to a window with tape, then placing one of the handmade sheets of paper on top. The light shining through the window allows you to draw over the lines using a felt-tip pen.

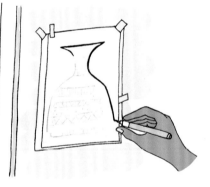

TIP
It is easy to adjust the dimensions of this project to suit the size of your jar. You just need to make sure that the paper is a little wider and a little taller than your jar.

3 Trim both pieces of paper to match the height of your jar.

4 Place the two pieces of handmade paper on top of each other, right sides facing out, and stitch together. Make sure both vases are the same way up! Using double thread, anchor the thread in place by starting with a few stitches on the same spot at the base of one of the sides, then sew the papers together with a simple running stitch along the side. Stitch a few times on the same spot at the top of the side to make sure the thread stays in place.

5 Repeat on the other side, then simply slide the paper cover over your jar.

Dyed GLASS

Changing the color of your glass vessels will really transform their appearance. Dye a whole collection of different shapes and sizes, then group them together on a wooden tray, as shown here, for maximum effect. Once dyed, the jars are no longer safe to use as drinking glasses or for food storage due to the varnish glue, but they work really well for displaying your favorite trinkets and flowers. You will need to use an oven for this project.

YOU WILL NEED:

glass jars and bottles in different shapes and sizes

disposable cups

old teaspoon

varnish glue, such as Mod Podge

food coloring

cardboard or newspaper

baking sheet

greaseproof paper or baking parchment

oven gloves

1 Wash the jars thoroughly and make sure all the labels and "best before" dates are scrubbed off (see pages 10-11).

2 In a disposable cup mix 4 teaspoons of glue with 2 teaspoons of water and 3 drops of food coloring (add more drops if you want a stronger color). Pour the mixture into a glass jar, swirl it around to make sure all the glass is covered, then tip the excess liquid back into the cup.

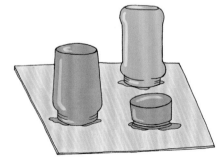

3 Stand the jar upside down on the cardboard or newspaper to let the excess color drip out. Leave to drain for about 10 minutes. Repeat to color as many jars as you wish. You may want to experiment with different strengths of color.

4 Preheat your oven to 225°F/110°C/gas ¼. Line a baking sheet with greaseproof paper, place the jars upside down on the paper, and slide into the oven. Leave to dry for 10 minutes.

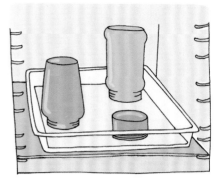

5 Wearing oven gloves, take the baking sheet out of the oven and carefully turn the jars the right way up (change the greaseproof paper if it is marked with color), then return to the oven for a further 20 minutes.

6 The jars are ready when all paint drips have disappeared. Let them cool before you use them.

TIP
I used a selection of glass containers for this project, including jam jars, drink bottles, cooking sauce jars, and a tea light holder.

Hanging LIGHT

I absolutely love this light! It combines my love for upcycling with a fresh pop of color and a modern industrial look. Electric flex encased in colored fabric is widely available nowadays—I really liked using this bright yellow as it contrasts so well with the black metal of the lampshade. You don't necessarily have to add a shade—just the jar on its own makes for a great light, especially if you group a few jars together. Don't attempt to do any electrical work unless you are a qualified electrician as it's better to be safe then sorry.

YOU WILL NEED:

cloth-covered electric flex with light fitting attached

large glass jar with a screw lid

felt-tip pen

drill and bit

metal cutters

black paint and paintbrush (or black nail polish)

old-fashioned Edison-style bulb

black metal lampshade that fits around the jar

1 As the hanging light is attached to a ceiling rose, you don't need to have a plug attached to the electric flex. If your flex doesn't come with a light fitting attached, ask an electrician to attach it for you.

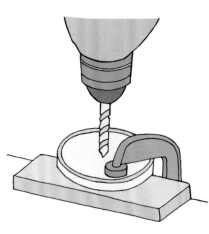

2 Using a felt-tip pen, mark the middle of the jar lid. Drill as large a hole in the middle of the lid as possible (see page 11).

3 Use metal cutters to enlarge the hole so that the light fitting on the end of the electric flex can fit through it. Take care as the snipped metal edges will be very sharp.

4 On each side of the central hole, drill two ventilation holes. These are needed to prevent the jar becoming too hot if the light is switched on for a long time.

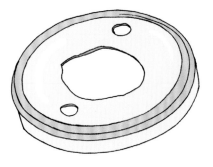

5 Paint the lid black, using spray paint (or do as I did and use nail polish— I had run out of spray paint!). Let dry.

6 Unscrew the two parts of the light fitting. Push the top part through the lid (make sure the top of the lid is facing upward). Screw the bottom part of the light fitting back on underneath the lid.

7 Screw the light bulb into the fitting, then place the bulb inside the jar and screw on the lid tightly.

TIP

You do need to use a very large jar for this project, as it's important that the glass doesn't become overheated by the bulb (I used a giant jar that had once contained pickles). For the same reason, it's also important to drill the ventilation holes in the lid.

8 Push the cord through the lampshade and have an electrician wire the light into your ceiling rose.

Cement VASE

Cement and concrete have been used in interiors for some years now—they are a great way to add an industrial feel to your home. Instead of pouring the cement into the jars (see page 28), here I've used it around the jars. Dig into your recycling bin for any plastic or wax-lined cardboard containers that have a good shape and which will comfortably hold the jars. I like using rapid-set cement but this does mean you have to work quickly when inserting the jars!

1 Using an old spoon, mix the cement powder in a bowl with water according to the packet instructions. The mixture should be the thickness of yogurt.

YOU WILL NEED:

old spoon

old mixing bowl

rapid-set cement mix

safety mask

safety goggles

plastic container
(I used a box which
once held laundry
detergent sachets)

glass bottles or
tall jars

paper towel

craft knife

fine sandpaper

2 Working quickly, pour a little of the mixed cement into the base of your mold, then tap the mold to get rid of any air bubbles. Place the glass bottles in the mold, ensuring they are straight.

3 Fill the mold with cement to your chosen height, gently tapping the sides of the mold to release any air bubbles. Use paper towel to wipe any cement splashes from the bottles.

4 Let the cement set. This can take anything from half a day to several days, depending on the type of cement used — follow the packet instructions.

SAFETY TIP
When working with a concrete mix, always wear a safety mask and goggles.

5 When the cement is completely hard, carefully cut away your mold using a craft knife. Use fine sandpaper to smooth away any rough edges, and then your vase is ready.

Chapter 3

DECORATE YOUR GARDEN

Tea light VOTIVES

These shallow glass jars started life as crème brûlée containers, but I've given them quite a makeover! Swirling them with different shades of nail polish has resulted in a tie-dye effect, and when the tea lights inside are lit, the flames enhance the colors. This is a really easy way to make votives to fit any theme or color scheme.

_1_ Gather together all your bottles of nail polish and create some pleasing color combinations. You need between two and four colors per votive.

YOU WILL NEED:

selection of
nail polishes in
different colors

plastic container,
such as a take-out
food container

small glass jars,
such as crème brûlée
containers

baking parchment

nail polish remover

cotton swabs

tea lights

_2_ Fill the plastic container three-quarters full with cold water and drizzle the nail polish in, making sure you create a pretty swirling pattern.

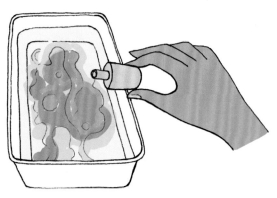

_3_ Holding the jar by the rim, carefully dip it into the container. Make sure that the rim stays clear of the liquid. The nail polish will immediately attach itself to the jar. Place the jar upside down and let dry for an hour (ensure the work surface is protected by paper — I use baking parchment as the nail polish doesn't stick to it).

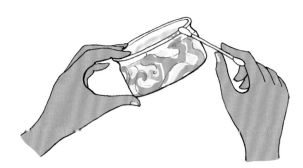

4 Dip more jars in the same plastic container if you want a matching set of votives, or start again with different color combinations. When the nail polish is dry, use a tiny drop of nail polish remover on a cotton swab to remove any smudges or spots where the polish has touched the rim

5 Paint the rim of the jar one solid color—it may require two or three coats of nail polish, but allow each coat to dry before applying the next. Pop a tea light in each finished votive.

Solar LIGHT POST

I love spending time in my garden, and this clever lighting idea works wonders in the evening, adding atmosphere and lighting the path. Encased in a post made from old floorboards, this light blends into the garden, but if you wish, you could paint the wood for a more contemporary look. Made from a garden solar spike light, one of the best things about this light is that it doesn't need any electricity. This project uses simple woodworking skills.

YOU WILL NEED:

pencil and paper

measuring rule

garden solar light

jar with an opening that fits the solar panel—I used a pasta sauce jar

wooden planks—I used two floorboards

drill with wood bit

jigsaw

sandpaper

chisel

hammer

masking tape

wood glue

wood screws

screwdriver

nails

Diagram labels: 4¼ in (11cm) · 2½ in (6cm) · 33 in (85cm) · 4 in (10cm)

1 Draw out your plan using this cutting guide as a template. You might need to alter the dimensions of the post slightly to fit your jar. You will need four uprights for the sides and a rectangle for the top. My side panels measured 4 in (10cm) wide, 33 in (85cm) tall, and ¾ in (2cm) thick. My top piece measured 4 x 5½ in (10 x 14cm).

2 Cut the pieces of wood to size. Remember to double-check all measurements before cutting the wood.

3 Remove the stem from the solar light (this is the spike you would usually push into the ground). This will leave you with the solar panel and the bulb below it. Check that this fits into the neck of the jar.

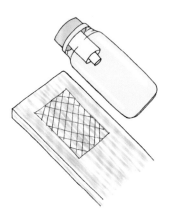

4 Place the jar on one of the side panels, with the top of the jar/solar panel roughly level with the top of the wood. Using a pencil, draw a rectangle on the wood to mark the position of the window. The window needs to be slightly shorter and narrower than the jar. The windows on my post measure 2¹/₂ x 4¹/₄ in (6 x 11cm).

5 Drill a hole in the window area to fit the jigsaw blade through, then cut out the window. Sand the rough edges around the window opening. Repeat with the remaining three side panels.

6 The insides of two side panels need to be shaped a little, to ensure the jar is held in position. Hold the jar in place on the window and trace around the base and top of the jar. Carefully remove this area of the wood to a depth of ¹/₂ in (1cm) by placing the chisel on the marked line and hitting it with the hammer to slide the chisel through the wood. Sand the rough edges. Repeat on a second side panel.

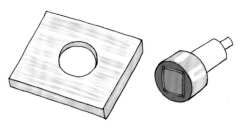

7 On the lid, draw a circle the size of the solar panel, making sure it is placed centrally in the lid. Cut out the circle, once again by drilling a hole to fit the jigsaw blade through. Sand the rough edges.

8 Push the solar panel through the hole in the lid, to check that it fits. Place the solar panel in the jar and stick the two together by wrapping with tape.

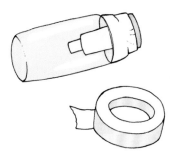

9 Now assemble your post. Measure and mark five evenly spaced holes down the front edges of the two side panels without the chiseling. As I used wood ¾ in (2cm) thick, I placed the holes ¾ in (1cm) from the outer edge of the panel. Pre-drill these holes.

10 The two panels with the wood carved out go opposite each other, against the inside of the other drilled panels. Apply wood glue to the edges of the chiseled panels, butt up next to one of the drilled panels, and screw in place. It helps to use masking tape to keep the panels together while screwing in place.

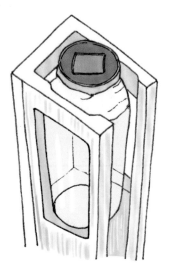

11 When three panels have been assembled, insert the taped-together jar and solar panel. Glue and screw the fourth side panel in place.

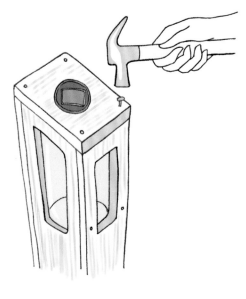

12 Place the lid on top of the post and nail in place.

Lantern JAR

When pruning garden shrubs, keep any straight twigs as they can be used very effectively in this project. The twigs I used for this lantern come from my elder tree and have an amazing texture—it looks like the twigs are covered in polka dots! The lantern is made from a medium-sized jar which originally contained pickles, but you can adapt the project to suit the size of your jar or the length of your twigs.

YOU WILL NEED:

glass jar

selection of straight twigs

secateurs or garden pruners

twine

scissors

tea light

1 Cut the twigs to the height of your jar plus approximately 2 in (5cm)—you need a little difference in the length of the twigs. Brush any dirt or dust off the twigs, and trim away any side shoots or leaves.

2 Cut two lengths of twine, each piece four times the circumference of the jar. Fold each piece in half.

TIP
If you only have short twigs to hand, decorate a tiny votive. If you have a large branch, make a big lantern with a glass vase to hold the candle.

3 Insert the first twig into the twine at the fold and tie the twine in a knot, roughly 1¼ in (3cm) from the bottom of the twig. Repeat with the other piece of twine, roughly 1¼ in (3cm) down from the top of the shortest twig.

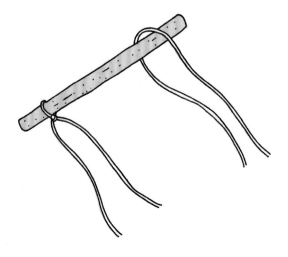

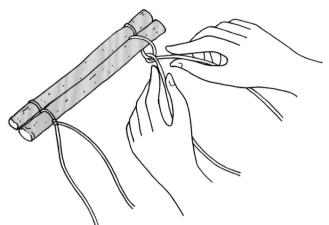

4 Line up the second twig next to the first. Make sure the bottom ends are even. Tie the twine around at the top and bottom of the second twig, as in step 3, knotting it tightly in place.

5 Continue attaching more twigs in this way, until the twig "mat" is long enough to wrap snugly around the jar.

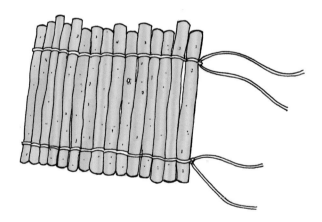

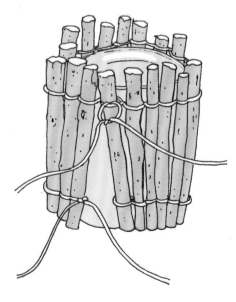

6 Stand the twig "mat" upright and wrap it around the jar. To keep the mat in place, loop the remaining ends of the twine tightly around the first twig. Knot in place and cut off the twine ends.

7 Pop a tea light inside the finished lantern (you will need long matches for lighting it).

Citronella CANDLE

I'm an outdoor person and love spending as much time as possible in my garden, on the beach, or in fields and forests, although this can mean being plagued with mosquitoes. However, the scent of citronella is known to repel these bugs, so I now light citronella candles to keep the insects at bay. Citronella candles are easy to make, either by melting down old bits of candle or by buying wax chips. In the winter, swap the citronella for a warm scent like coffee or cinnamon.

1 Place the wax chips or the candle ends in an old saucepan and melt very gently over a low heat. (An average size jam jar holds 9 oz/ 250g of wax, but I have also made smaller candles in glass ramekin-style jars.)

YOU WILL NEED:

9 oz/250g candle wax chips or leftover ends of old candles

old saucepan

electric hotplate

2 pencils

2 rubber bands

wick, slightly longer than the depth of the jar

jam jar

2 teaspoons citronella candle fragrance

scissors

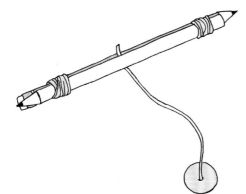

2 Tie the pencils together at each end using the rubber bands. Thread one end of the wick between the pencils (this will make sure the wick stays upright in the middle of the jar, rather than dropping into the wax as it sets).

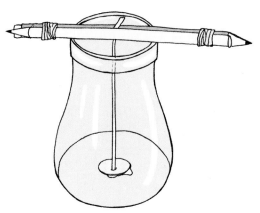

3   Place the wick in the bottom of the jar, with the pencils resting on the rim of the jar. You can secure the wick in place by dipping the bottom in the melted wax before lowering it into the jar.

4   When the wax has melted completely, add the fragrance to the saucepan. Use approximately 1 teaspoon of fragrance per 3½ oz (100g) of wax —here I used 2 teaspoons for a standard sized jam jar.

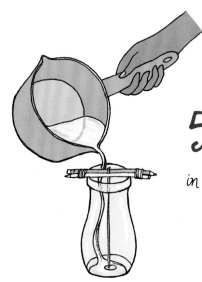

5   Carefully pour the most of the wax into the jar, leaving a few teaspoons of wax in the saucepan. Leave the wax to set.

6   When the candle has hardened, it is likely that the top surface will be lumpy or uneven due to air bubbles released near the wick. Reheat the leftover wax and pour into the jar to even the surface. Let it cool.

7   When the candle has set, remove the pencils and trim the wick to a length of ½ in (1cm).

TIPS

Candle-making fragrances are widely available online (as are wax chips and wicks). Always make sure the perfume you buy is safe to use in candles as you don't want to create a fire hazard. The safest way to melt the wax is on an electric hotplate. Don't let the wax get too hot and never leave the melting wax unattended.

Bird FEEDER

Bring some style into your garden with this great bird feeder made from a Mason jar, a bottle stop, a broomstick, and an old plate. This is upcycling to the max! The glass keeps the birdseed dry, and you can easily refill the jar by lifting the bottle stop. Just like birdwatching, this project isn't for the less patient amongst us. The holes on the rim that distribute the seeds take some time to cut out, as does the big hole for the bottle stop. However, the project is well worth the effort and your little feathered friends will be very happy with you!

YOU WILL NEED:

broomstick

drill, with wood and ceramic bits

ceramic dinner plate

masking tape

pencil

screw

screwdriver

large Mason jar, or similar (I used a 33 fl oz/945ml jar)

rotary cutter with a diamond drill bit

bottle stopper

strong glue suitable for outdoor use

birdseed

1 First, make the feeder stand. Pre-drill a hole in the middle of one end of the broomstick.

2 Drill a hole in the middle of the plate. Place a small strip of masking tape on the back of the plate and mark the position of the hole on the tape. Fit your drill with a ceramic drill bit if you have one (a normal drill bit may also be used). Place the plate on a suitable surface and carefully drill the hole.

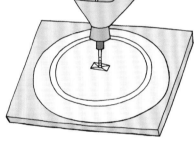

TIP
Remember to protect the work surface when drilling the plate so that it is not damaged by the drill bit. I like to use my work bench.

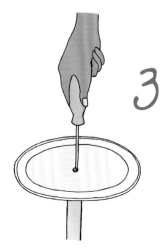

3 Screw the plate securely to the top of the broomstick.

4 Drill a hole in the bottom of the Mason jar, big enough to fit your bottle stopper. This will take a while to do as the bottom of a jar is always thicker than the sides. Follow the glass drilling instructions on page 10 and don't rush the drilling as you don't want to break the glass.

5 Using the rotary cutter, drill three equally spaced semi-circular indentations around the rim of the jar. This will also take some time as the rim is thick. Make the indentations large enough for the birdseed to fall through. When you have drilled, test the size of the indentations by putting the jar upside down on a plate and filling it with some seeds. Check that the seeds will go through the holes and enlarge the holes if necessary.

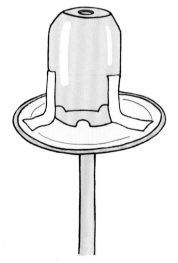

6 Push the base of the broomstick into the ground so that the plate is horizontal. Put some strong glue around the straight edge of the jar rim and press it centrally on to the plate. If you wish, hold the jar in place with strips of masking tape until the glue has dried.

7 Remove the masking tape when the glue is dry. Fill the jar with birdseed through the top hole, add the bottle stopper, and wait for the birds to arrive.

Tiki TABLETOP TORCH

This tiki torch oil lamp makes a great addition to your outdoor table, adding extra light when the sun goes down or bringing atmosphere to a garden party. Even if you have limited table space, there is always a spot for this Mason jar. It creates the perfect centerpiece and brings a welcoming ambience to your backyard and patio. If you don't have a garden, you can fill the torch with a lamp oil which is safe for indoor use.

YOU WILL NEED:

Mason preserving jar, or similar

drill

metal cutters

copper reducing coupling piece (available from the plumbing department of a DIY store)

copper spray paint

length of wick, the same thickness as your coupling piece (mine is ½ in/1cm)

lamp oil

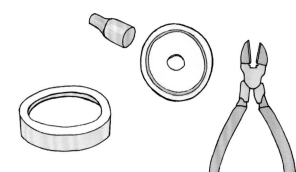

1 Drill a hole (see page 11) in the lid of the jar large enough for the narrow end of the coupling piece to fit through. If you don't have a large enough drill bit, use metal cutters to make the hole bigger.

2 Spray paint the lid copper (see page 11). These jars often come with a two-part lid, so spray each piece separately. Let dry.

3 Push the narrow end of the coupling piece through the top of the lid.

4 Cut an 8-in (20-cm) length of wick and push it through the coupling piece. The wick needs to be long enough to lie on the base of the jar and soak up the oil.

SAFETY TIPS

Don't place the torch under trees or overhanging branches or near flammable fabrics.

Never leave a lit torch unattended, and make sure it is out of the reach of children and pets.

Use a candle snuffer to extinguish the flame.

Store the jar upright so that the oil does not spill out.

5 Fill the jar a quarter full with the lamp oil. Place the wick in the jar and screw the lid closed.

Chapter 4

GIFT IDEAS

Skyline CANDLE

Unleash your inner artist and draw a cityscape to surround a jar, turning it into a great tea light votive! Draw your own street, your favorite vacation spot, or a make-believe fairytale town. Don't worry if you think you are not creative enough to come up with your own design—simply copy my Amsterdam cityscape from page 125. Acetate is great to draw on and any area not covered in pen will let the candlelight shine though. Acetate pages are used in those old-fashioned overhead projectors and as binding covers, and can be found in stationery shops.

YOU WILL NEED:

cityscape design, or use the template on page 125

small sheet of acetate (it needs to be large enough to wrap around the jar)

sticky tape

felt-tip pens—I used ones with black and copper ink

scissors

small jam jar

tea light

1 Copy the template from page 125 or design your own. The template is for a small jam jar—if you use a bigger jar, you might need to enlarge the design or repeat some of the houses.

2 Place the acetate on the template. You may wish to hold it in place by sticking it to the paper with small pieces of sticky tape. Copy the outline of the houses using the black pen.

3 Color in parts of the houses, but keep some of the windows clear to allow the light to shine through. You can give the houses details such as bricks or weatherboarding, or give them an all-over color.

4 Cut the design to match the height of your jar
(cut in a straight line, don't follow the house
shapes). Wrap the acetate around your jar and stick
the two edges together with a strip of tape applied
vertically. Add the tea light and your votive is ready.

Cookie mix in a jar

When visiting a friend for dinner, it's nice to bring a little gift but instead of the traditional flowers or bottle of wine, why not take this jar of cookie mix? Everybody loves cookies and your host can whip up a batch whenever they fancy just by adding butter and an egg. Write the recipe on a label and attach it to the neck of the jar. I call this recipe "Gone before you know it cookies" as whenever I bake these, my friends nibble them up immediately. They taste good fresh out of the oven, but I prefer them the next day. Once the ingredients have been tipped out of the jar, you can use it to store the cookies!

YOU WILL NEED:

25 fl oz (750ml) lidded jar

1¾ cups (250g) self-rising flour

½ cup (100g) brown sugar

½ cup (100g) M&Ms, roughly chopped

½ cup (80g) dark chocolate chips

brown paper label or piece of paper

pen

twine

You want defined layers of ingredients for a clean look. Start by pouring the flour into the jar, then flatten the top of it with a spoon.

Carefully spoon the sugar on top of the flour and level it. Then it's time for a layer of M&Ms, followed by the chocolate chips. Clip or screw your lid in place.

To make the label, on the front write the name of the cookies or your message to your friend. On the back write down the recipe:

"Preheat the oven to 350°F/175°C/Gas 4. Mix all the ingredients together with ⅔ cup (150g) soft butter and 1 egg. Roll into a log and cut into discs ¼ in (5mm) thick. Place on a baking sheet and bake in the preheated oven for 15 minutes or until golden."

Tie the label around the jar with some twine.

QUICK IDEAS

Snow globe SPICE SHAKERS

As a child, you may have made a snow globe out of an empty jar, but did you know you can use the same technique to make these unique spice shakers? These little guys definitely bring a sense of fun to your table setting and you can match the little ceramic animals with the "landscape" they live in. For example, here I have a polar fox in the salt shaker so he appears to be playing in the snow, a meerkat sits in the ground pepper which resembles sand, while the beaver is playing in a forest of fallen leaves made from dried chili flakes. You can also use little ceramic houses, trees, or even plastic model figures.

YOU WILL NEED:

small ceramic ornaments (mine are from Green Owl Studio on Etsy)

small jars with screw-top lids

spray paint

rotary cutter with a diamond bit

safety goggles

superglue

craft foam and scissors (optional)

ground pepper, salt, and chili flakes

1 Make sure your chosen ornaments fit into your jars easily. Scrub the ornaments in hot water to make sure they are spotlessly clean, then let dry.

2 Paint the lids with spray paint (see page 11), inside and out, and let dry completely.

3 Drill the holes in the bottom of the jars (see page 10). You will need small holes for the pepper and salt and a slightly bigger one for the chili flakes. Wash the jars thoroughly to remove any glass dust.

4 Place the animal ornaments inside the lids and glue in place. Before gluing, if you find they disappear behind the jar rim too much, you can give them a height boost by gluing a circle of craft foam to the lid, and then gluing the animal to the foam. Let the glue dry.

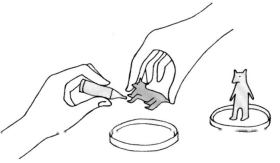

5 When the glue is completely dry, fill the jars one-third full with your chosen spices. Cover the hole in the base of the jar with your finger as you do this, to prevent the spices coming out. Screw the lids on tight, then stand the jars on their lids. The spices will settle around the animals, creating a cute scene.

Birthday IN A JAR

With everything you need for a party wrapped up in a jar, this is the ultimate birthday present! Find a jar that fits your present, then make a birthday crown and pom-pom bunting, sprinkle in some confetti, and add some birthday candles. Everything the birthday boy or girl needs, whatever their age!

YOU WILL NEED:

jar with a screw lid

tissue paper

small wrapped present (that fits inside the jar)

birthday confetti

birthday candles

FOR THE BUNTING:

40 in (1m) cord, twine, or yarn

8 ready made pom-poms

needle and thread

scissors

FOR THE CROWN:

template (see page 124)

sheet of paper

medium-thick yellow felt

fabric marker pen

ruler or tape measure

scissors

2 buttons

needle and thread

FOR THE LID:

giftwrap paper

pencil

scissors

varnish glue and brush

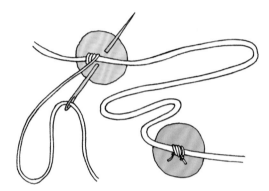

1 To make the bunting, cut a 40-in (1-m) length of cord, twine, or yarn. Sew the pom-poms to the twine, spacing them out evenly and keeping 4 in (10cm) free at each end, for tying the bunting in place. You can, of course, make the bunting longer if you wish.

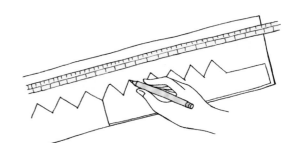

2 To make the crown, trace the template on to a piece of paper and cut out. Trace the outline on to the felt; when you reach the end of the template, simply flip it over and keep tracing until the crown reaches the desired length. These are the average lengths I use, but you can adapt them to suit the recipient: man 22½ in (57cm), woman 21½ in (55cm), child 19½ in (50cm). Cut out the felt.

3 Make two slits in the felt on the end that has the crown points (these slits will form buttonholes for fastening the crown). The start of the first slit is ½ in (1cm) from the edge of the felt, the start of the second slit is 2 in (5cm) from the edge. Each slit should match the diameter of the buttons.

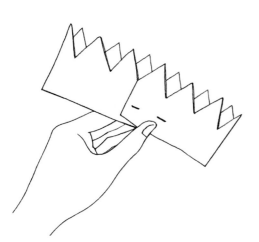

4 Fold the crown into a circular shape. Mark on the flat tabbed end of the felt, through the button holes, where the buttons will be. Make sure that the points of the crown on the overlap line up.

5 Sew the buttons in place. The crown now fastens to different sizes—for a smaller size, use both buttons and buttonholes; for a larger size, just use the end buttonhole and the end button.

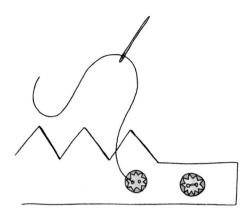

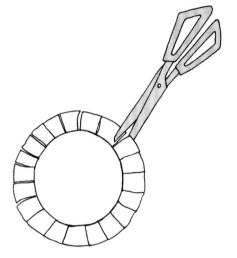

6 To decorate the lid, use the same giftwrap paper used to wrap the present. Draw around the lid on the wrong side of the paper, then draw a second circle 2 in (5cm) larger. Cut out the larger circle and make little slits toward the smaller circle. This makes it easier to wrap the paper around the sides of the lid.

7 Cover the lid with glue and place the paper on top, right side up. Fold the snipped edges around the sides of the lid and glue in place. Apply one more layer of glue on top of the lid. Let dry.

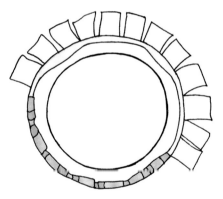

8 To assemble, add some tissue paper to the jar. Fold or roll the crown into a circle and place in the jar. Place the present in the middle of the crown. Drape the bunting around the present and scatter confetti on top. Place birthday cake candles around the crown, then screw the lid in place.

Labeled STORAGE JARS

We probably all use glass jars for food storage, so wouldn't it be fun to make them look more stylish? Updated with just a simple decal, any recycled jar will deserve to take pride of place in your kitchen. Use a computer to play around with different typefaces and designs. You will need to print your words on special decal paper, but make sure you buy the right type of paper for your printer—there are different papers for inkjet and laser printers.

YOU WILL NEED:

jars with lids

spray paint (optional)

computer and printer

printer paper

scissors

washi tape

glass decal paper (also called glass transfer paper)

1 Spray paint the lids of the jars if necessary (see page 11), and let dry.

2 Create your labels. Experiment on your computer with different typefaces and layouts, until you have a label you are happy with.

3 Decal paper is expensive so you don't want to make any printing mistakes. First print a test piece on normal paper, cut the label out, and stick to your jar with some washi tape. You can now see if the label is the correct size and you can adjust your computer document accordingly.

4   When you are happy with your design, print on the
    decal paper following the instructions on the packaging.
Make sure you print on the correct side of the paper. Let the
labels dry for at least 10 minutes, then cut them out.

5   Peel off one third of the protective film
    and place the label on the jar. Gently
press out all the air bubbles using your fingers.
Slowly peel the remainder of the protective film away
and remove the air bubbles for a neat finish.

Cake in a jar

I love using glass containers for cakes and have done so for years. The jars make the cakes look great, are portable, and you don't have to bother with plates—just add a spoon and you are ready to eat. You can use recycled jars like jam and chutney jars, or use small Mason or Kilner preserving jars, as I've done here.

This simple cake is one of my favorite bakes. Filled with juicy blueberries and with blueberry frosting, it is cake heaven. When making the frosting, remember that the longer you whisk, the fluffier it will be. With the lids closed, these cakes keep in the fridge for 3 days.

YOU WILL NEED:

1¾ cups (325g) butter, at room temperature

⅔ cup (125g) superfine/caster sugar

2 eggs

2 cups (250g) self-rising flour

⅓ cup (100ml) milk

1 teaspoon vanilla extract

3 cups (300g) blueberries, plus extra for decorating

3 cups (400g) confectioners'/icing sugar

electric mixer

8 x 8 in (20 x 20cm) cake pan, lined with baking paper

stick blender

6 small glass jars (mine are 8¾ fl oz/250ml)

Preheat the oven to 350°F/175°C/Gas 4.

Make the cake. Using an electric mixer, cream ½ cup/125g of the butter with the superfine/caster sugar until light and fluffy. Add the eggs one at a time and mix until incorporated. Add the flour, milk, and vanilla extract; mix until the flour is incorporated. Spoon through half the berries. Pour into the cake pan. Bake for 20 minutes or until brown on top. Cool on a wire rack.

Make the sauce. Place the remaining berries in a saucepan, add 2 teaspoons of water, and cook for 5 minutes. Take off the heat and use a stick blender to make a smooth sauce. Let cool.

Make the frosting. Mix the confectioners'/icing sugar with the remaining butter for 5 minutes. Add the cooled sauce and mix for 30 seconds. Spoon into a piping bag.

Cut the cake into ¾ in (2cm) cubes. Pipe a dollop of frosting into the base of the jar, then add a layer of cake, pressing it into an even layer. Top with frosting, then repeat the layers to the top of the jar. Decorate with blueberries to finish.

QUICK IDEAS

Chapter 5

STYLISH STORAGE AND DISPLAY

Wall-mounted VASES

I found these vintage preserving jars in a thrift store a while ago and had been wondering how to use them—I think this project is just the right solution. I have these wall-mounted vases hanging on an outside wall so I can add a few pretty blooms to my seating area. As well as using it for flowers, you could use it to store kitchen utensils such as wooden spoons, or hang it by your desk for all your pens and pencils.

YOU WILL NEED:

piece of wood, such as an old floorboard, measuring 16 x 8 in (40 x 20cm)

paint and paintbrush (optional)

measuring rule

pencil

2 D-ring picture hangers

small screws

screwdriver

2 hose clips, 3-4 in (80-100mm) in diameter

drill with a metal bit

2 Ball Mason or Kilner preserving jars, 3½ in (9cm) in diameter

small nails or hooks, for hanging the vases

1 If you wish to paint your piece of wood, do this first. You may need to apply two coats of paint.

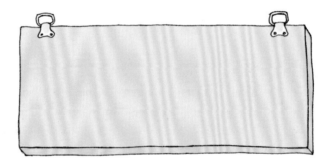

2 On the back top edge of the wood, measure in 2 in (5cm) from each side and mark the spot with a pencil. Screw the picture hangers to the back of the wood at these two points.

3 Use a pencil to mark the central point on the hose clips, directly opposite the clasp. Drill a hole through each hose clip at this point.

4 Screw the hose clips to the front of the wood, making sure they are an equal distance from the sides.

5 Slide one of the jars into a hose clip. Using a screwdriver, close the hose clip screw as tight as you can to ensure the jar is secure. Repeat with the second jar, then hang from a couple of nails or hooks screwed into the wall.

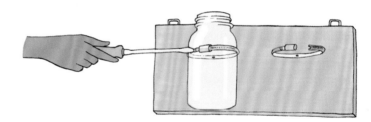

TIP

The hose clips used here can be found at plumbing suppliers or home improvement stores. They are available in different sizes, so you could make this project using smaller jars and smaller clips.

Jewelry STORAGE

This jewelry stand will keep all your necklaces, bracelets, and rings sorted, while the clear glass makes it easy to see what's inside. The two-tone triangle gives a nice graphic edge to this organizer.

If you have a lot of jewelry, you could make the stand larger by adding more jars. Alternatively, use the organizer in your kitchen and fill with dried herbs or pulses, or in a child's room to store crayons and other craft supplies. Wherever you need some extra storage, these jars will sort you out.

YOU WILL NEED:

measuring rule

rectangular piece of wood or medium-density fiberboard for the front, 12 x 8 in (30 x 20cm)

triangular piece of wood or medium-density fiberboard for the stand—the two right-angled sides each measure 5½in (14cm), the long side 8in (20cm)

pencil

drill with a wood bit

masking tape

paint in two colors (I used gray and coral)

paintbrush

screws

screwdriver

filler

filling knife

sandpaper

3 small jars with screw-on lids (I used jam jars)

2 metal cup hooks

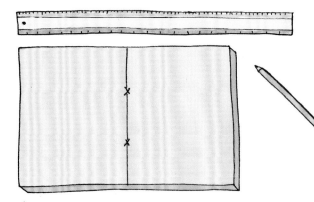

1 Using a measuring rule, find the middle of one of the long edges of the rectangular piece of wood. Draw a vertical line from this point down to the bottom edge of the wood. Measuring up from the bottom, make two pencil marks 3¼in (8cm) and 4¾in (12cm) from the bottom edge. These two points are where you will attach the stand with screws. Drill a hole at each point, large enough to accommodate the screws (so that the screw heads will sit below the surface of the wood).

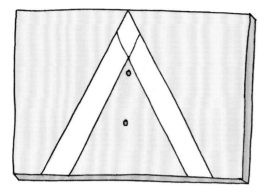

2 Now decide the size of the triangle to be painted on the front. Draw the lines in pencil first, then place masking tape just inside the pencil lines.

TIP
I drew a triangle with three equal sides, but you could use different shapes or dimensions if you wish.

3 Paint the area outside the triangle gray. Also paint the edges and back of the rectangular piece of wood and the stand. Allow the paint to dry. Apply a second coat if necessary and let dry.

4 When the paint is dry, remove the masking tape. To attach the stand, line the stand up behind the pre-drilled holes and screw in place.

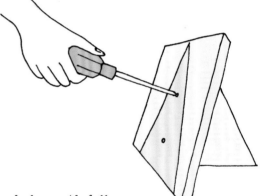

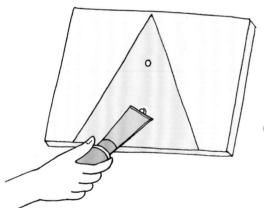

5 Fill the screw holes with filler and let dry. Sand the surface of the filler smooth.

6 Drill a hole in the middle of each jar lid (see page 11). Space them evenly on the central triangle, then screw in place.

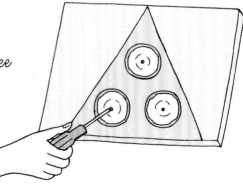

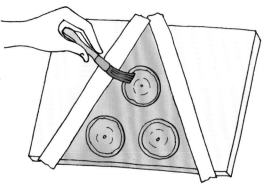

7 Paint the inside of the triangle and the jar lids in coral. You might want to put masking tape on the edges of the triangle to make the painting easier. You will probably need two coats of paint, especially on the lids. Let dry, then remove the masking tape.

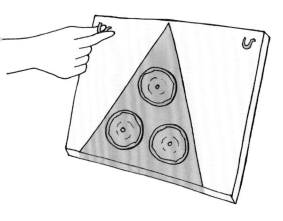

8 Screw the cup hooks into the wood, close to the upper corners.

9 To use, fill the jars with your jewelry and screw on to the lids. Hang shorter items from the hooks.

Kitchen storage jars

These stylish kitchen food containers look expensive, but in fact they are simply empty jars which have been given a makeover. The advantage of using glass storage jars means that you can instantly see the contents and do a stock-check of what's in your pantry. And while there is nothing wrong with a sturdy clip-top jar, how about creating something more exciting? Something you can show off on open shelving? And the great thing about using spray paint to decorate the lids means that you can easily change the color whenever you wish.

YOU WILL NEED:

empty jars with screw lids

plastic coral (the type used in aquariums, usually available from fish or pet stores)

superglue

spray paint

Gather together your materials and create a safe space for spray painting. I like doing this outside, against some paper taped to the wall. If using spray paint indoors, make sure you open windows and doors for a well-ventilated room (see page 11).

Use a drop of superglue to attach the coral to the center of each lid.

When the glue is dry, apply a light coat of spray paint and let dry. Apply a second coat of paint, for even coverage and to help prevent the paint chipping during everyday use.

When dry, fill your smart new storage jars, screw on the lids, and display in your kitchen.

QUICK IDEAS

Dome JAR

This is a really inventive way to reuse your empty jars—turn one into a glass dome! Put a favorite trinket on display, or use the dome like a mini glasshouse for growing small cacti and succulents. You might even want to make one that will house the key to your first home, your wedding cake topper, or your baby's first pair of shoes. Whatever is special to you will look amazing displayed in this way.

YOU WILL NEED:

jar wide enough to cover whatever you want to display

wooden base wider than your jar—I used a tree slab

pencil

rotary cutter

superglue

large wooden bead

1 Decide whether you want the dome to sit centrally on the wooden base or to one side. Place the jar in the desired position and trace around it with a pencil.

2 Using your rotary cutter and following the pencil outline, carefully create a groove ¼ in (5mm) deep and very slightly wider than the rim of your jar. Remember that you need to cut just inside the pencil outline. Brush the sawdust away. Check the jar sits in the groove; if not, cut away a little more wood.

3 Use a drop of superglue to attach the bead to the top of the jar. Allow the glue to set, then place the dome on the wooden base.

TIP

The dome is kept in place by a groove cut into the wooden base which stops the glass from sliding. If you don't have a rotary cutter you can skip this step, but just be a little more careful when moving your dome around.

Vacation memories in a jar

Instead of displaying your favorite snaps in photo frames, pop them in a jar! Did you go on a beach vacation? Take some sand, shells, or driftwood back home with you and place these in the bottom of the jar. Did you go on a city escape? Why not fill the base of the jar with coffee beans from your favorite espresso bar and pick up some small trinkets or save tickets to decorate the jar with.

QUICK IDEAS

$\mathcal{Soap}$ DISPENSER

I'll let you in on a little secret—I used to have fancy dishwashing liquid on display when guests visited, but as soon as they left, the cheap stuff came back out and the fancy bottle disappeared into the cupboard! Plastic detergent bottles are not the prettiest things to look at, but that's history now with this great Mason jar dispenser. It takes you just 5 minutes to make (you'll need to recycle a dispensing pump from a hand-soap bottle), but it will make your kitchen sink look so much better!

YOU WILL NEED:

pump dispenser from an empty bottle, such as a hand-soap bottle

Mason jar, or similar

drill

metal cutters

superglue

masking tape (optional)

scissors

1 Take the pump out of an empty hand-soap bottle and wash it to remove any build-up of soap.

2 Drill a hole in the middle of the jar lid (see page 11), large enough to fit the pump. If you don't have a drill bit of the right size, drill three smaller holes and use metal cutters to join them up into one big hole.

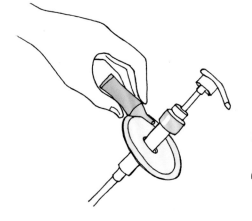

3 Push the pump through the hole. Glue it in place with superglue, holding it in position until the glue has dried. Alternatively, stick a length of tape over the pump to hold it steady while the glue dries.

TIP

I like the dispenser in its original steel color, but if you wish you can spray paint the lid to match your kitchen decor. Be careful to give the pump dispenser only one light coat of paint and when it's dry, top with a coat of clear gloss or varnish. The moving part of the pump piece might lose its paint during use if the paint is applied too thickly.

4 When the glue is dry, place the lid on the jar—you may need to snip a bit off the pump tube if your Mason jar is shorter than the original soap bottle. Fill the jar with dishwashing liquid and screw the lid on tightly.

Etched jar

Page 44
Either use at this size,
or adapt to suit the size
of your jar

Templates

Paper vase cover

Page 62
Either use at this size,
or adapt to suit the size
of your jar

Skyline candle

Page 94
Enlarge by 200%,
or adapt to suit
the size
of your jar

Resources

JARS

Ball Mason, Weck, and Kilner jars can bought from most homeware or kitchen stores. Online, have a look at:
www.lakeland.co.uk
www.walmart.com
www.kilnerjar.co.uk
www.weckjars.com
www.freshpreserving.com

Fairs, thrift stores, charity shops, and yard sales are also great places to pick up old jars. The foreign food aisles in the supermarket are great for finding more unusual jars. Milk bottles can be found in antique shops and I also like using empty Starbucks frappuccino or Snapple bottles. The table light is made from a milk-style bottle from Ikea, www.ikea.com.

PAINT

I like using Kobra spray paints as they come in great colors and you often only need to apply one coat.
www.kobrapaint.co.uk

I also love the milk paints of General Finishes—beautiful colors and super easy to apply.
www.generalfinishes.co.uk

For a matt or distressed finish, I like using the chalk paints of Annie Sloan. They don't require any preparation such as sanding and priming—love it! www.anniesloan.com

DIY

I always have a look at the wood I have left in my shed before purchasing anything new—you'll be surprised at what you can make from offcuts or leftover cupboard doors. Local lumber yards are also great, or try one of the big superstores:
B&Q www.diy.com
Homebase www.homebase.co.uk
Home Depot www.homedepot.com

A rotary cuter makes working with glass very easy. I think the Dremel tool does the best job and you can get a lot of different attachments, so you can use it on metal, wood, and tiles as well. www.dremel.com

The light cable and fittings used in this book are from Vendimia Lighting Company, as are the vintage-style Edison bulbs. www.vendimialighting.co.uk

CRAFT SUPPLIES

I love using Sharpies for drawing the vase cover and the candle surround. They are also great marking cutting lines. www.sharpie.com

Glue guns with a fine tip are great to "write" with, as in the vase project. You can pick them up at www.staples.co.uk or www.therange.co.uk

Handmade paper can be bought in craft supply shops or try www.khadi.com—they have a great selection.

Food colorings can be found in kitchen supply shops and in large supermarkets.

John Lewis is brilliant for fabrics, haberdashery, and general craft supplies. www.johnlewis.com

I love using Mod Podge varnish glue, which you can easily buy online or try www.michaels.com and www.hobbycraft.co.uk

I bought the paracord used on the vase on eBay, where there is a brilliant selection of colors and you can buy it by the meter. www.ebay.co.uk or www.ebay.com

Avery glass decals can be ordered online at www.avery.co.uk or bought from office supply shops like Staples, www.staples.co.uk

INTERIORS AND HOMEWARES

Anthropologie sell the best quirky home accessories and artefacts from around the globe. www.anthropologie.com

I love West Elm—they make it very easy to decorate your home in a modern, chic way with ethnic touches. www.westelm.com

For a bit of Dutch influence, I like the designs of Hema. They sell everything you ever need in your life, from cool home decorations to stationery (including the best washi tape) at very affordable prices. Shops can be found in every town in Holland, but luckily for us they also ship abroad. www.hemashop.com

For budget-friendly textiles, go to H&M Home. A lot of the photo props in this book came from there. www.hm.com

I found the little ornaments in the terrariums and spice shakers on Etsy—a great website for anything unique and handmade. The spice shaker ornaments are from Green Owl Studio. www.etsy.com/uk/shop/GreenOwlStudio

HESTER'S SOCIAL MEDIA

www.hestershandmadehome.com
twitter.com/hestershandmade
www.instagram.com/byhestergrams
www.facebook.com/hestershandmadehome

WEBSITES AND MAGAZINES

There is so much inspiration to be found online or from magazines. I'm a bit of a magazine junky, and as you can read foreign magazines online now, my obsession is only getting worse. Here are some of my favorites.

www.pinterest.com I love browsing everyone's pins for tips and ideas.

www.instagram.com It's amazing that you can have a glimpse inside the lives of crafters and makers all over the world. There are some amazing interior shots to be seen.

www.sweetpaulmag.com I love the magazine and website of Sweet Paul, always full of amazing ideas and tips.

www.westelm.com Click on the link to read the great interior blog of West Elm.

www.kinfolk.com I'm slightly obsessed with the slow-living lifestyle of Kinfolk magazine. If you haven't read their magazine yet, pick one up now!

www.brightbazaarblog.com Will has a keen eye for color and will make you want to transform your home into a beautiful paradise.

www.abeautifulmess.com Elsie and Emma have such a fresh and unique approach to home decor and crafts—their projects just make you smile.

www.vtwonen.nl Dutch interior and craft magazine which gives you a great look at toned-down Dutch design.

www.clementinecreative.co.za/ideas-magazine/ The South African Ideas magazine is packed full of craft tips and ideas.

www.thesimplethings.com An obsession of mine since their first issue, this magazine is all about taking time to live well and enjoy the small things in life.

www.marthastewart.com The queen bee of crafting, what's not to love. Martha's Living magazine should be on every craft and lifestyle lover's reading list.

www.flowmagazine.com If you are a lover of paper, creativity, and mindfulness, there is only one magazine for you.

www.bhg.com Go to Better Homes and Gardens for the amazing Do It Yourself magazine.

www.countryliving.co.uk Great furniture ideas and inspiration.

SHOOT LOCATIONS

The book was photographed in Hester's house and in Little Stour Orchard www.littlestourorchard.co.uk

Acknowledgments

A big thank you to the lovely people of CICO Books, especially Cindy Richards for giving me a second book to work on, my great editors Anna Galkina and Gillian Haslam for making sense of my written word, and designer Geoff Borin for his great design talent. A huge cheer for James Gardiner and his fantastic photography—it's always so much fun shooting with you. Thank you to Jasmine Parker for replying to my tweet request so I could discover your amazing talent—your artworks complement my projects perfectly.

Thank you to Ian for all your help and for saving every glass jar that passed through our house.

Micky and Sarah of Little Stour Orchard—thank you so much for letting me use your amazing orchard as a shoot location, and Micky for your wiring lessons and endless supply of apple juice.

And last but not least, a big thank you to my mum and dad—they are the best DIY advisers.

Index

Chapter 1
PARTY TIME

Drinks DISPENSER

Filled with home-made lemonade or a fun cocktail,
this beautiful drinks dispenser will add an element
of vintage charm to your party, and your guests will
be so impressed you made it yourself. Using a jar
with a wide neck and a clip-top lid makes it easy
to add ice, fruit, and herbs to the drink.

YOU WILL NEED:

large jar with an easy-to-open
lid (I used an 8-pint/4-liter
clip-top preserving jar)

waterproof marker pen

old towel

protective goggles

rotary cutter with a diamond
drill bit (ideally cordless—
see Tips overleaf)

cooling gel (see Tips overleaf)

drinks dispenser faucet/tap

1 Mark the position of the faucet/tap on the jar
with a waterproof marker pen. It needs to be
approximately 2 in (5cm) above the base of the jar.

2 Place an old towel in the sink to keep the jar in
place. Wearing protective goggles, set the rotary
cutter to low speed and drill a hole in the marked
place. Don't apply any pressure to the drill. Keep the
glass cool by running water over the cut, spraying it
with water, or adding the cooling gel on the cut.

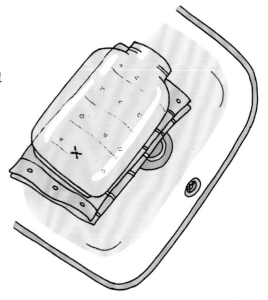

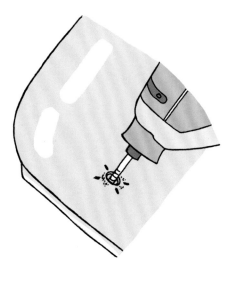

3 When you have drilled through the glass, you need to enlarge the hole so that the faucet/tap will fit. Widen the cut by wiggling the drill bit around the cut. Don't apply pressure and work slowly until the hole is big enough.

4 Wash the jar thoroughly to remove all the glass dust.

5 The faucet/tap should be supplied with seals and a nut. Put one of the rubber seals on the faucet/tap and push it through the glass, add the other seal to the end inside the jar, and tighten the nut. It's tricky using tools inside the jar, so do this with your hands.

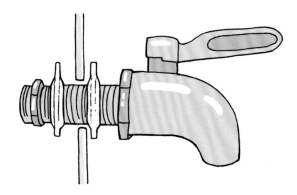

TIPS

I used a cordless rotary cutter with a diamond bit to make the hole in the glass. It's a good idea to practice your cutting skills on an old empty bottle first, but as long as you follow the guidelines and safety rules you will find drilling glass isn't as tricky as you may think.

Always wear protective goggles, drill on a low speed, don't put pressure on the drill, and keep the glass cool with water or a cooling gel. I find it easiest to drill glass in the kitchen sink— I place an old towel in the sink to keep the jar in place and stop every minute or so to pour water over the hole to reduce the chance of the glass overheating and cracking. The water also prevents glass dust flying up. If using an electric cutter (rather than a cordless one), use a spray bottle of water or a cooling gel instead of running water.

Floral table arrangement

I love using jars to display flowers, and have been known to select brands of drinks and preserved food purely based on how pretty the jar or bottle is. I find myself looking at supermarket shelves in a completely different way, shopping for jars and bottles, rather than their edible contents.

I enjoy creating flower arrangements and have developed this easy way of making big statements with little expense. When buying flowers, look for blooms with colors that go well together, such as yellows and whites, purples and blues, or soft tones with one accent color. Or opt for a theme and use only meadow flowers, or herbs, or, as here, flowers with a tropical touch.

YOU WILL NEED:

jars in different shapes and sizes

glass tea light holders

selection of foliage, such as leaves and herbs

selection of flowers—some large "statement" flowers and some smaller "filler" flowers

Arrange the jars and tea light holders in a long line down the middle of your table. Fill these "vases" with water.

First, arrange your foliage and herbs in the jars. I like using sprigs of rosemary and mint picked from my garden, mixed in with a few bought leaves in different shapes and shades of green.

Add the big statement flowers. Try to have the tallest flower in the middle jar of your line and the shortest ones at the ends. Add the smaller flowers to the smaller jars.

Finish your arrangement with little pops of color wherever needed. I also used some single flowerheads in shallow glass tea light holders.

QUICK IDEAS

QUICK IDEAS

Storage for knives and forks

When setting a table in an informal, rustic style, it's great to use empty jars to store knives and forks and napkins. Placed in the middle of the table, everybody can easily grab their own knife and fork when the food arrives. Any tall jars with wide necks would be perfect for this quick make.

Tea light HOLDER

Candlelight brings instant atmosphere to a gathering and just a few tea lights dotted around in glass jars can really create a cozy feel without too much effort. I love these jar candle holders on their long sticks—they are super easy to move around the garden, you can line your path with them for a special welcome, or arrange them around outdoor seating. I used ten of these lights to decorate a friend's beach party, dotted all over the sand, marking out our party area and creating a feel-good mood.

YOU WILL NEED:

Ball Mason preserving jar, or similar

binding twine

long bamboo stick

scissors

glue (optional)

fresh flowers, for decoration (optional)

handful of small gravel

tea light

long matches

1 Remove the lid from the jar.

2 Wrap a long piece of twine around the top of the bamboo stick, about 2 in (5cm) from the top and with the ends of the twine even. Secure the twine tightly around the bamboo with a firm knot.

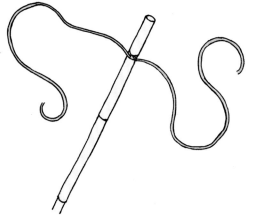

3 Place the neck of the jar on the top of the knot, wrap the twine around the jar, cross in the middle, and double knot the twine at the back of the jar.

4 Wrap the twine tightly around the jar again, this time bringing it to the back around the bamboo pole. Secure with a double knot. Repeat the wrapping and knotting until the jar feels securely attached to the bamboo.

5 Cut off the leftover twine. Screw the outer metal ring of the lid on to the jar.

6 To attach the bottom of the jar, wrap a long piece of twine around the bamboo and tie with a double knot. Wrap the twine around the lower part of the jar and double knot at the back. Repeat this twice and cut off any leftover twine. If the bamboo pole or jar is a bit slippery and the twine doesn't grip, apply a small dot of glue between the twine and the jar.

TIP
I used a Ball Mason preserving jar, which has a two-part metal lid—a flat metal circle and a screw-top ring to hold the lid in place. However, you could easily use any jar of a suitable size.

7 To use, push the bamboo stick firmly into the ground or the sand. Tuck fresh flowers into the small gap between the jar and the bamboo if you wish. Add a handful of gravel to the jar, pop a tea light on top, and light with a long match.

Picnic in a jar

Load up a basket full of jars filled with tasty treats and set off to the countryside for a delicious picnic. Packing individual servings of food into jars makes it easily portable, and also means that you don't need to take plates and serving bowls.

When packed into jars, delicate foods avoid being squashed in the bottom of a bag. For extra comfort pack a picnic blanket too—if placed on top of the jars, this will serve the dual purpose of preventing the jars from rattling around in the basket. You can keep everything cool by putting some plastic bottles of frozen water in your basket.

Here are some of the foods I like to pack for a picnic:

* Fragile snacks like potato chips/crisps and pretzels are great to keep in jars as this prevents them being smashed into crumbs in transit. You also don't need a serving bowl —just pass the jar around.

* Layered salads look great in jars. Make a graphic looking salad by layering up brightly colored vegetables. Start with a layer of watercress, top with chopped tomatoes, then add a layer of sweetcorn, and finish with some sliced radishes.

* Soft fruits, such as strawberries or raspberries.

* Instead of baking cinnamon buns on a baking sheet, drop the mixture into a glass jar, then bake as specified in your recipe.

* Cake in a jar (see my recipe on page 106).

* Thick American-style pancakes are great for stacking in jars. Use the rim of the jar to cut circles out of your pancakes. Smear jam on top of the circles and alternate them in the jar with whipped cream and raspberries.

* Add some bottles of fruit juice for the perfect feast.